I0765866

Snowflake Generation

Lionel Bolnet

Author and self-publisher:
Lionel Bolnet

Distributor:
www.lulu.com

Table of Contents

Foreword... 6

Definition... 10

Humor 25

Resilience... 35

Cultural appropriation 44

Their children 48

Anti-snowflakes 51

Sources.. 53

The Author... 58

Foreword

Far from seeking to set young people against old people or adults against teenagers, Western sociologists want to study the behavior of human beings and compare them with their parents. At the beginning of the twentieth century, the German sociologist and philosopher Wilhelm Dilthey defined generation as: "A fairly narrow circle of individuals who, despite the diversity of other factors involved, are connected in a homogeneous whole by the fact that they depend on the same major events and changes that occurred during their period of receptivity." This definition, in simpler terms, means that most human beings born within a range of years will tend to develop similar behaviors. Being a child during the First World War, during the conquest of space or during the heyday of Facebook inevitably impacts the behavior of future adults. Admitting that generations exist and that they are different is the first step towards a tolerant and balanced society. Knowing which generation you belong to allows everyone to understand why their behavior is not dictated by their will alone. Understanding the generations helps to improve or strengthen human interactions, whether they are between parent and child, between colleagues, between neighbors or even between company and customer.

Children born between 1890 and 1925 are collectively referred to as the "Lost Generation". It was lost under two different meanings: on the one hand, the word lost refers to the fact that they lacked landmarks in a changing America or Europe. On the other hand, the generation that lived at that time lost part of its youth because of the First World War. Ernest Hemingway, André Malraux or Salvador Dalí are part of this generation.

The "Silent Generation" is that which was born between 1925 and 1942. This generation was born between the Great Depression and the Second World War. It is known for working hard and not being assertive, hence its name. It includes people (especially for the United States) who fought in the Korean War. Its members are characterized as fatalistic, conventional, with a random moral sense, expecting the worst but remaining hopeful. Included in this generation are: Martin Luther King Jr. Elizabeth Taylor or Silvio Berlusconi.

A "baby boomer" is a person born in the West during the baby boom period after the Second World War. Therefore, a baby boomer is generally considered to be a person born between 1946 and 1964. They have a very strong character. They are hardworking but admit to enjoying leisure and pleasure, especially food and sex. The music of their time, rock, represents them well: protestant but not anarchist. The baby boomers are the first generation to distrust and distance themselves from religions. 33% of them have never set foot in church. They are narcissistic but at the same time very supportive and have implemented most of the civil rights movements. The next three American presidents are baby boomers: Bill Clinton, George W. Bush and Donald Trump.

The "Generation X" is as follows: Children born between 1960 and 1976 were born in the midst of social transition, at the beginning of the decline of colonial imperialism and during the Cold War. This generation experienced a low point in their professional life, finding it difficult to find stable and well-paying jobs. The new forms of generational precariousness are specific to it. According to Strauss and Howe's classification, this generation is "nomadic", which explains its taste for adventure, its cynicism and its counter-culture that opposes the baby boomers. Generation X seems to have been supplanted (in the interests of business) by Generation Y and can sometimes be presented as its adversary. Famous X's are Kurt Cobain, Sergey Brin (founder of Google) or Barack Obama.

In the West, "Generation Y" includes all those born between 1980 and the year 2000. Perceived as having their own sociological and behavioral characteristics, they are a particular target in the field of marketing. They have not had to endure the threat of the Cold War apocalypse. They have not known the world without AIDS. They were young enough at the time of the massive introduction of consumer computing to have acquired an intuitive mastery of it that generally surpasses that of their parents. However, they have experienced computing without the Internet. They were born with the beginnings of the general public's interest in ecology (which was previously the concern of a minority). For them, video games are commonplace entertainment, unlike Generation X, for whom it was still sometimes perceived as marginal. Generation Y likes to have fun, is not assiduous at work, communicates easily, shares emotions easily and doesn't stand still. Famous Ys include Mark Zuckerberg, Lady Gaga or Emma Watson.

Finally, the "Generation Z" is the one that was born from 2000 onwards. They are also called the "Millennials". Some of them are major this year (2018, date of writing of this book). They have always known terrorism, globalization and the Internet. According to Nicolas Sadirac, founder of EPITECH and general director of the 422 school, Generation Z has "an uncomplicated relationship with error! For them, it is normal to make mistakes: they do not demonize failure like other generations". Some of them are just beginning to be known, such as dancer Maddie Ziegler, Willow Smith (daughter of Will Smith) and actress Quvenzhané Wallis.

Generations Y and Z are the constituents of the Snowflake Generation.

Definition

The term "Snowflake Generation" is a neologism inspired by a single short sentence from the book and film "Fight Club" (1996 for the book, 1999 for the film). This sentence is "You are not a beautiful or unique snowflake".

Fight Club tells the story of a nonconformist man who organizes, in a basement of a building, clandestine fights open to all, for men who want to evacuate their discomfort through violence. In the film, the manager of the clandestine club, with the help of a megaphone, shouts at his members: "Listen up, maggots. You are not special. You are not a beautiful or unique snowflake. You are the same decaying organic matter as everything else". The sentence means that every man is mortal and perfectly equal to another.

In January 2017, the author of this novel, Chuck Palahniuk says he has coined the term "snowflake" to designate a generation of young adults who express a kind of neo-Victorianism. To understand the term Victorianism, one has to go back to British society between 1780 and 1850. Under the reign of Queen Victoria (1837-1901), England abruptly ceased to be an aggressive, brutal, violent, heckling, outspoken nation and became an inhibited, timid, polite, orderly, prude and hypocritical nation. This transformation, called "Victorian morality", has the good taste of reducing cruelty to animals, criminals, madmen and children. At the same time, this wave of prudishness imposes on British society strict moral codes such as sexual abstinence, self-censorship and fear of nudity.

At the beginning of 2010, it is the return of this form of softening of morals that leads several sociologists and authors to question themselves. Why are the young adults of the 2010's so cautious, fragile, offended by anything?

The term snowflake is a good translation of the concept. A snowflake has three undeniable characteristics:

- It is beautiful,
- It is fragile because it can melt easily,
- It is unique.

According to several sociologists, the children born from 1980 onward were, in spite of themselves, raised in a family bubble that instilled in them the idea that they were beautiful, exceptional, brilliant, unique and destined for a bright future. Who told them this? On the one hand, the parents of the 80/90s and on the other hand, society in general: the media, the press, advertisers.

Let's start with the parents. From time immemorial, children were simply collateral damage to the life of a couple, an accident caused by sexuality. The child, once integrated into the family, was quickly raised to become a responsible adult. He was silent when grown-ups spoke and obeyed. He was a satellite of his parents and not a Sun. The child once knew very well what their adult life would be like because they had the model right under their nose. They participated in household chores and helped their father with certain tasks. Without necessarily being mistreated, the child was not put on a pedestal. All this model changed from the second half of the 20th century.

In Canada and the United States, the term "helicopter parent" refers to a parent who "hovers" over their child to direct them to the best possible future, or who flies to their child's rescue when a problem arises. These parents are very involved in school life, very close to their children and excellent counsellors to help them through the various stages of childhood. Unable to say no, they do not teach their children how to manage frustration. The existence of these parents would be caused by two factors: Western society expects them to be friends of their children rather than guides, and maintains a high level of competition that encourages parents to constantly participate in their children's success.

The 1990s played a very special role. Precisely between the fall of the Berlin Wall and the September 11 attacks, the 1990s is a period of optimism in the West. Globalization is on the rise, there are no more major wars, and money is king. Most parents in the 1990s are better off than when they were children themselves. Televisions are in color and are on from morning to night, with no competition from other devices (no internet or smartphones). This color television is not insignificant: we know that children are more attracted by colors than by black and white. Advertisers are having a field day: they literally flood children with toy commercials. The adults of the 90s, the first to invent the term child king, no longer know how to resist their children's pressing desires. The commercial system is well organized: television is the first agent provocateur, then children's catalogs and newspapers are the second. Finally, shopping malls and supermarkets finish off the parent! His kid has already seen the same toy advertisement 100 times. The parent is at Toys'R Us, he can no longer turn back because he sees dozens of other parents queuing up: he has to buy, he has to give in. The best part is that, thanks to the progress of globalization, children's toys are not very expensive, which makes it easier for the parent to give in to the pressure of his offspring.

It is not only advertising or marketing that has generated child kings. The appearance of the contraceptive pill in the 1960s changed the way we look at children. From a random burden, the child becomes "desired". That is to say that from the 1960s on, adults decide whether they want a child or not. When the child arrives, he is already known, he already has a first name, his room is already painted blue or pink and we even know the approximate shape of his face. This child, if programmed, if desired, if expected, will necessarily benefit from parental attention at all times. There will never be any question of "letting them cry" or letting them throw a tantrum. It is since the 90s and even more so today that the debate "for or against letting a baby cry" rages. While for millennia, parents all over the world have been letting babies cry (even those who were hungry or whose diaper was dirty!), in recent years, the press and the internet have been bombarding parents with headlines like "5 reasons not to let baby cry" or "Top 8 reasons not to let your baby cry". Thus, the child takes the ascendancy over the adult as soon as he is born!

Parents in the 90s developed a "Special Snowflake Syndrome": it consists of having the conviction that their child is special and much more important than another. It can also be called the Parent Magazine Syndrome. Steeped in good intentions, magazines for young parents have been making snowflakes for years: they tell confused parents how to educate their children but, in doing so, they focus parents' attention on their children. What should have been a succession of wise advice becomes a champion preparation program. "Boost his immune system for the back-to-school season", "Our coach's advice", "Can we still give them ham?", "Your baby is a genius", "We can decipher his/her crying" are the headlines in this type of press. And all this accumulates above a blanket on which thrones a picture of a perfect baby whose Photoshop retouching time has been longer than the life of the child who served as the model.

In short, the parent has the impression that he or she is the smartest and most beautiful child on this planet and that, for this reason, his or her adult life is going to go like a charm!

On a broader field, the recent society has begun a softening of morals on several points and this is to be welcomed. We can cite at least ten "struggles" led by Western society since the 1980s:

- The fight against racism,
- The protection of children,
- The protection of the environment,
- Acceptance of overweight people,
- Assistance to the disabled,

- The acceptance of homosexuality,
- Assistance to the destitute,
- Assistance to developing countries,
- The fight against all physical violence,
- The protection of animals.

These movements were non-existent or embryonic until the mid-1980s. Then, they grew considerably from year to year. To get an idea of the novelty of these fights, let's take a few dates.

The fight against grossophobia began in the 1960s and 1970s in the United States. A "fat-in" (from sit-in and fat, big) took place in New York in 1967 and the National Association to Advance Fat Acceptance (NAAFA) was founded in 1969. In France, the association Allegro Fortissimo was founded in 1989. It is intended to fight against the discrimination suffered by people of large stature.

In 1971, France created a Minister of Ecology for the first time.

In 1976, the Society for the Protection of Animals (SPA) submitted the "animal charter" to the National Assembly, supported by Roland Nungesser, who later became one of the presidents of the association. In 1982, it starts the publication of the Animaux Magazine, which allows it to carry out campaigns on a larger scale. In 1987, a parliamentary study group for animal protection was set up in the National Assembly thanks to Roland Nungesser, its president at the time.

Band Aid is the name of the Anglo-Saxon group created in 1984 on the initiative of Bob Geldof and Midge Ure, to help the victims of the famine that was then raging in Ethiopia.

We Are the World is a charity song recorded by the American supergroup USA for Africa in 1985. It is written by Michael Jackson and Lionel Richie, and co-produced by Quincy Jones and Michael Omartian on the album We Are the World. The single aims to raise funds to fight famine in Ethiopia. The historic event brings together some of the most famous artists in the American music industry at the time.

Touche pas à mon pote (Don't touch my buddy) is the official slogan of the French association SOS Racisme. It was launched during the 1985 SOS Racisme concert.

Founded by Coluche in 1985, Les Restos du cœur, an association recognized as being of public utility, "aims to help and provide voluntary assistance to the underprivileged, particularly in the area of food, through access to free meals, and by participating in their social and economic integration, as well as in all action against poverty in all its forms."

On July 10, 1987, promulgation of Law No. 87-517 in favor of the employment of disabled workers (JO No. 160) which instituted for companies with more than 20 employees the obligation to employ, full or part-time, 6% of them. AGEFIPH (Association Nationale pour la Gestion du Fonds pour l'Insertion Professionnelle des Personnes Handicapées) was created to manage the fund for the integration of disabled people.

The rights of the child are a branch of human rights aimed at the specific protection of the child as a full human being. They are the subject of several national and international treaties, the most important of which is the Convention on the Rights of the Child (CRC), adopted by the United Nations General Assembly on 20 November 1989.

In 1990, the World Health Organization removed homosexuality from the list of mental illnesses. On November 15, 1999 in France, the parliament passed the law on PACS, a form of civil union granting certain rights and duties to both homosexual and heterosexual couples, while maintaining a universal spirit.

There is therefore a body of evidence of a collective awareness of the social and environmental struggles that began in the 70s and 80s, with a strengthening in the 90s and 90s. And this is very good!

But the problem is that these struggles have lastingly stigmatized terms, words. Entire concepts have become taboo. There is a before and after for many terms in everyday life.

Let's take the word "Black". This is a word that should refer to a person whose skin is dark and/or who has African physical features. The term, in itself, is not insulting. But in the 80s, it was necessary to accustom the French population, especially white people, to accept the blacks present in society. The anti-racist movement of the time wanted to indicate, and rightly so, that a black man should not be treated differently from a white man, whether by the police, his employer, his neighbors or anyone else. The flip side of the coin is that for all those children born in the 80/90s, the French word "Noir" has become a taboo in France. To replace it, the English word "black" has come to their rescue. And, by the way, Noir and Black are not the same person! A Noir is a victim of racism who has dark skin, whereas a Black is a normal young Frenchman who looks like Will Smith.

In an article in Libération dated December 10, 2007, journalist Catherine Mallaval explains how the political correctness of the 1990s and 2000s led to the deletion of terms that have become too shocking today. For example, "oceanizing a boat" replaces "sinking a ship, or other waste, which we want to get rid of."

There is also the term "surgical strike" which has replaced "battle", "persons with reduced mobility" to replace the horrible word "handicapped", "visually impaired" for "blind", "surface technician" for "janitor". The expression "cash register hostess" gives more shine to the cashier's job. When companies lay off employees, they "restructure". When people are unemployed, they become "active job seekers" and when someone commits suicide on the subway tracks, it is called a "traveler incident".

This fashion of flattening the words made the French people who saw them smile, but pissed off their parents. But the generation that was born inside finds this vocabulary quite normal. They are the snowflakes. They have been so protected from the outside world that even their vocabulary is wrapped in bubble wrap to prevent them from hurting anyone.

But all this sentimentality could have gone unnoticed without an invention that appeared at the beginning of the 21st century: social networks.

- On February 4, 2004, Mark Zuckerberg founded Facebook.
- On March 21, 2006, Jack Dorsey founded Twitter.
- On October 6, 2010, Kevin Systrom founded Instagram.

Social networks are the microscope of contemporary society. Thanks to them, anyone on this planet can hold a podium and give their opinion out loud. With Twitter in particular, Barack Obama or you and I have the same weight. Anonymous citizens can shoot down a personality or demolish the reputation of a brand or a film. If social networks didn't exist, snowflakes would often be offended, but in silence. Instead, they whine in front of the world.

On January 8, 2018, the multinational company H&M will include a green hooded sweatshirt in its catalog with the inscription "Coolest Monkey in the Jungle" in white letters. The phrase means "Coolest Monkey in the Jungle". Yes, but on the website, the little boy wearing the sweatshirt is black. The outcry is immediate. On the social networks, the chain store is flooded with messages of indignation, the young people insult H&M and use the term they prefer for all occasions: "Racist!" For those who don't speak snowflake, let's analyze what happened. First of all, there is the inscription: it contains the word "monkey". This animal has a negative connotation that a tiger or partridge, for example, would not have. Secondly, the child is black, and the insult of calling black people monkeys is an old habit that has indeed been the habit of racists for centuries. Worse, it's a hooded sweatshirt, a symbol of an unattractive suburban youth, often of immigrant origin. In the popular imagination, the hooded sweatshirt worn by a white person means he is a computer hacker and worn by a black person means he is a suburban rioter.

The "Coolest Monkey in the Jungle" case was very damaging for the brand. Under the flood of criticism, the brand was forced to apologize publicly and withdraw the sweatshirt from sale. Why is this case a snowflakery? Well, because it contains all the distinctive elements:

- Amalgam between a serious case and a light case without incidence,
- Social networks,
- Self-censorship and public apology by the company.

However, the fight against all forms of racism does not lie in the inscription of a banal sweatshirt.

Luckily, the snowflake generation knows how to make fun of itself: in the months following the affair, several smart guys with a sense of commerce bought back the stocks of the unfortunate garment to resell it on eBay, sometimes 2,000 euros each! Since then, other similar sweatshirts have been produced by other companies in order to surf, by provocation, on the wave of this affair.

As early as January 13 of that same year, the mother of the little boy seen wearing the sweatshirt on the H&M website, Terry Mango, spoke up and said, "I am the mum and this one of hundreds of outfits my son has modeled... stop crying wolf all the time, unnecessary issue here...get over it!"

What's worse is that the over-representation of blacks and browns in advertising is precisely a subterfuge that companies have adopted to give themselves an image of an open-minded society. This is called "blackwashing", literally "going through the black process". Nowadays, try the exercise: go to five websites of famous companies and look at the color of the person you see first.

H&M advertising is just one small example in the mass of "withdrawn advertising" over the last five years. The two most frequently used reasons are "advertisement deemed racist" and "advertisement deemed sexist". Unable to understand the underlying messages of the posters, the younger generation screams, storms and whines at every advertisement that shocks them. At one time it was enough not to look at the poster, but nowadays they "demand the removal" of the object in question and get it. Youth have even found a term for their tendency to see racism and sexism everywhere. They call it "ordinary racism" and "ordinary sexism". It means "I'm shocked because there's a black guy in this chicken ad" or "Help, there's cleavage in this ad.

In 2004, Häagen-Dazs chose to show a black woman eating dark chocolate ice cream and a white woman eating white chocolate. The snowflakes almost had a heart attack.

In 2007, processor manufacturer Intel showed a white man satisfied with the performance of its employees: they were caricatured by black sprinters. Their posture is that of athletes preparing to start a race, so they are bent back, leaning on their hands. The snowflakes see this as a form of submission of the black man to the white man.

2016. Advertising for GAP clothing. A young white girl leans on her friend, black. The scene is seen as "a black girl is serving as an elbow rest for a white girl". The Internet goes up in flames and Gap is forced to apologize. Ironically, a year earlier, an almost identical Gap ad went completely unnoticed, except that it was the black child who was elbowing the white girl's head...

In May 2016, the Chinese laundry brand Qiaobi features a black house painter that an excited Chinese woman puts in her washing machine. The young man comes out clean as a penny ... and Chinese. Let's not be blind: what is shocking is the idea that a black man is no longer black after a wash. Is the skin color of a black man dirt? But why should we not take it so badly? For one thing, this is not a Western advertisement. It's a Chinese advertisement and the very fact of meeting a black house painter is a fiction over there. Secondly, it's an advertisement designed to extol the merits of washing powder; a product whose main function is to make clothes white. The line is therefore forced to illustrate the power of the washing powder. If we take a good look at the young woman's eyes: even before putting the black in the machine, she already seems extremely excited sexually by the painter. So where is the racism since she shows no disgust towards the black character? This case is therefore the brutal encounter between the lack of tact of some and the lack of intelligence of others.

Advertisers want to shock us with all this. So, what if they do?! Shake it off guys! They're advertisements: they're meant to catch the eye and the commentary.

We wanted to make them aware but, in the end, they are too sensitive. These young people, who were told not to be racist, sexist, polluting, scornful, homophobic, understood everything well, or rather, understood too well. This education has had two collateral victims: humor and resilience.

On March 15, 2018, the first show of the new season of American Idol on ABC Channel, recorded in the fall, begins airing. The show features Benjamin Glaze, then 19 years old, who was auditioned by the jury composed of Katy Perry, Lionel Richie and Luke Bryan. Before this boy from Oklahoma begins his song, the jury asks him, in reference to Katy Perry's hit released in 2008, if he has ever kissed a girl. Benjamin Glaze answers with a smile, "No, I've never had a girlfriend". Then Katy Perry, 33, asks him to approach the jury table and, with a humor typical of this kind of show, offers him his cheek to kiss her, before surprisingly kissing her on the mouth. The young man keeps smiling but seems troubled, and then delivers a mediocre performance. On the Web, American snowflakes are going wild! Katy Perry's kiss is considered sexual harassment. The singer is even compared to Harvey Weinstein (a producer well-known to abuse his power over women in the entertainment world). The young man himself does not understand the outrage. He admits that he was uncomfortable but does not feel sexually assaulted.

Humor

If there's one discipline that has been at the expense of snowflake education it's humor. The dictionary tells us that humor, in the broadest sense, is a form of mocking wit "that seeks to emphasize the comical, ridiculous, absurd or unusual nature of certain aspects of reality".

Raised in the midst of the serious subjects mentioned above, an entire generation finds itself unable to laugh, because it believes that to laugh is to laugh.

You have to understand them. When you tirelessly explain to them that you have to respect everyone regardless of their looks, how do you expect them to laugh at a sketch by Coluche or the Inconnus?

In the 90's, Didier Bourdon, Bernard Campan and Pascal Légitimus, better known as the troupe "Les Inconnus", regularly mocked the French society. The France of the time, laughs out loud. Everyone goes through it: policemen, hunters, doctors, West Indian nurses, suburban youths, variety singers... Les Inconnus humorously underline what everyone has already seen in their lives. Their talent makes it possible to laugh without stigmatizing anyone. In the sketch "L'hôpital" (At the hospital), the three men are disguised as West Indian nurses: face and body blackened with shoe polish, they exaggeratedly mime the supposed nonchalance of the French overseas population by walking slowly, hands resting on their hips. With a stereotypical Caribbean accent, the three comedians (one of whom is the son of a West Indian) lean, without insulting, on the cliché of the black mama who works in the public services. At the time, the French, including the West Indians, laughed at this sketch.

Today, forget that sketch. No television station would dare to broadcast it. Why not? It has become "racist" in only twenty years. It contains everything that is forbidden by the "new moral order": the waxing, still called Blackface, the false accent and the nonchalant gait. The worst of the three is "Blackface", which in French is "grimage en Noir" or "black make-up", an American theatrical form of make-up practiced in minstrel shows and then in vaudeville, where a white actor plays a stereotypical caricature of a black person. After growing in popularity in the 19th century in the United States, blackface distinguished itself from the minstrel show and became a practice in its own right at the beginning of the 20th century, until it disappeared in the 1960s following the African-American civil rights movement.

In 1976, Coluche puts on black makeup in one of the characters he portrays in his cult sketch mocking the Schmilblick; this sketch is known as The Schmilblick.

In 1988, the humorist Michel Leeb made himself up in black in the theater play "Tenor".

Why was this black face in black not serious in the 80's when it is so badly seen nowadays? The reason lies in globalization and associations. It's the sulphureous history of blackface in the United States that finally came to France. When Coluche wears black makeup, the French don't know the history of this practice and simply understand the humorous side of it. But nowadays, the influence of America is very strong and even without having a problem with blackface, we are impacted.

The other cause of the scandal is the activity of minority defense associations. Their work might seem noble, but it is a long time since they have fallen into a form of dictatorship of thought and even of good thinking. The CRAN, the Representative Council of Black Associations in France, for example, like other associations of the same kind, poses as a fuel for the snowflake generation. On any occasion, they rise up and demand the censorship of such and such a work, such and such a publication.

On March 22, 2014, the TV columnist Valérie Bénaïm disguises herself as a singer of "La Compagnie Créole" before arriving on the set of the famous TV show, Touche Pas à Mon Poste (Don't touch my television). In order to look like a Caribbean woman, the young woman had her face made up in dark brown. The outcry was immediate. It is one of the first blackface scandals in France. The little snowflakes that attack her on social networks are simply French people imitating young Americans.

On December 27, 2017, following the publication of the poster for the new edition of the Reunionese Fantastic Film Festival, "Même pas peur" (Not even scared), showing two Siamese women painted in black, its director, Aurélia Mengin, is accused of blackface by CRAN, who asks her to withdraw her poster and threatens her with legal action. This example is very serious because it shows how moral censorship is making a comeback by using the courts as an instrument.

Again in 2017, the player of the French soccer team, Antoine Griezmann, provoked an outcry by publishing a photograph of him grimly dressed in an Afro wig and dressed as a New York basketball player. On social networks, the scandal is total: users of Twitter, Instagram or Facebook, i.e. mostly young people born after 1980, are outraged. The snowflakesphere can't digest the fact that a white man disguises himself as a black man. Yet it is only humor. Standing, dressed in basketball outfit (they are often black), he holds a ball in his hand. His posture is dignified and he specifies well in the legend, that he is going to a costume party whose theme is "80's party". The tribute is therefore not recognized as such but is confused with insult. These young people therefore lack humorous education.

In the United States and France, other incidents that could be called "snowflakeries" have occurred in recent years. All cultures ask that we stop imitating them: Chinese, Japanese, American Indians, Polynesians...

The time when children were dressed as a little Chinese girl, a Hawaiian dancer or a Heidi is over! If you take the initiative to pay tribute to the beautiful red silk dresses of Chinese women, you are a racist. If you are white but you braid your hair, you are a racist.

We can no longer even distinguish between what is racist and what is not. In 2013, following its successful film "Frozen", Disney is accused of glorifying the beauty of white women. Yet four years earlier, after the release of "The Princess and the Frog", which features a young black heroine, the African-American community was outraged by the representation of blacks in the feature film.

In 2016, Disney reiterates its tribute to cultures around the world with Moana but still faces misplaced susceptibility. One of the main characters in the film, Maui, is directly inspired by one of the great figures of Polynesian mythology. When the first images of the film are released in June 2016, the appearance of Maui, represented as obese, arouses a lot of criticism from Polynesians who consider this graphic choice as the revival of an insulting and discriminatory cliché (assimilated to "fat-shaming", comic mockery against overweight people), in a region where problems related to obesity are frequent.

Sometimes the younger generations no longer understand each other! Thus from 1994 to 2004, a mythical, unavoidable series, Friends, made millions of young people laugh with its 236 episodes. The series educated the young people of that time (probably born between 1982 and 1992) by tackling subjects as varied as love, friendship, sexuality, fame, betrayal, pride, work, family, homosexuality, parenthood, money, music, success, failure, self-confidence, flirting, stress management, solidarity, health, pregnancy, death, rejection, obesity, sports, embarrassing situations, animals, food, obsessive-compulsive disorder, divorce, unemployment or infertility.

The series hasn't been on the air for years, when Netflix decided to put it in its catalog in 2017. And then the shock: a new generation finds itself in front of Friends. Snowflakes watch this series broadcast at the time of their birth and are nauseous. For them, Friends would be sexist, homophobic, transphobic and even grossophobic. Maladapted to the concept of humor, badly educated by overprotective parents, influenced by current struggles such as the fight against discrimination, young people born after 1990 do not understand the series. It's not that they don't find it funny; it wouldn't be very serious. No. They are shocked. British young people, in particular, feel uncomfortable with the episodes of this series. Ross is described as homophobic by those who don't understand the narrative of the series: this character is bitter towards his ex-wife because she married a woman after their divorce.

Chandler is also pointed at because when Joey takes him in his arms, he makes a face that is considered "homophobic". As if we can't accept homosexuality and not like male hugs.

According to Cosmopolitan magazine, for Joey, "every woman is a conquest before being a human being". In several episodes, he considers women as objects. In the first episode of the series, Joey compares women to "ice cream flavors" and he invites Ross to "grab a spoon". The problem with this highly flirtatious character that is Joey is that, nowadays, affairs such as DSK, Harvey Weinstein or Trump's vulgar behaviors have changed the deal in the relationship between men and women. In the 90's, Joey was a flirty clown because it was believed at the time that the relationship between men and women was healthy.

But in 2017/2018, with the excesses denounced by the #MeToo and French equivalent #BalanceTonPorc (expose your pig) movements, this relationship is catastrophic! Let's be clear: it is not the fault of the current generations if the relationship between men and women is bad. We should even point out the average age of the men targeted by the wave of sexual harassment complaints: they are generally men who are well over 40 years old. The movements to denounce sexist men or aggressors are not snowflake whims. On the contrary, they are indispensable steps to eradicate the feeling of impunity. But we have to take things into account: Joey's character in Friends or Barney's character in How I Met Your Mother should not be taken for what they are not. They are seducers, not aggressors.

The snowflake generation will have to learn to distinguish between the gravity of a fight and the lightness of an artistic or humorous production. It would be a terrible lack of intelligence to lump Harvey Weinstein and Joey Tribbiani together. The younger generation cannot just be outraged at everything they see. If they are, it is a failure of previous generations. In the Friends series, Monica is a character who overcame obesity as a teenager to become a skinny young woman. Under no circumstances should we believe that the passages that evoke her obesity are grossophobic episodes. On the contrary, it is the courage to face obesity and the gaze of others that is the moral of this series. Saying that Friends is a grossophobic series is therefore a shortcut to be avoided.

Finally, the famous series is qualified as racist for the sole reason that all the main characters are white.

This, in contrast, did not shock anyone when the series The Cosby Show or Family Matters only featured African-Americans. By conspiring against a series full of white people, snowflakes themselves become racist. In reality, the supposed whiteness of the Friends characters never appears in the script of the series: the actors may be white in the image, but nothing in the story reinforces this fact.

The cursor of what is tolerable in terms of humor is moving up a little more every day. We are witnessing a Dieudonnization: the development of an intolerance to a form of humor, overnight. Even if we hate the way Dieudonné's words turned out, we must recognize that the anti-Dieudonné movement is the first act of controlling our laughter. For the first time, with this affair, at the end of 2013, the French government, led by Manuel Valls (not a snowflake at all since he was born in 1962), is telling the French what is humor and what is not.

What must be realized is that every area of the mind is gradually being banned. Creativity is being extinguished. Snowflakes are not actors of censorship; they are its victims. Who's at the controls? Subsidized media, politicians, community leaders and social networks.

The direction that French society is taking is the progressive reduction of freedom of expression under the weight of the censorship organization called Twitter.

But what are they laughing about then? The younger generation is not angry with humor, but they don't want to hear anything more that is a "trigger", that is to say, a trigger of discomfort. For example, a modern-day comedian cannot afford to pull on the outer edge of his eyes to imitate a Chinese man, nor can he evoke Mimie Mathy's waist or wear a rasta wig.

In any case, to follow a comedian's show, you already have to be concentrated, something this generation is not very capable of.

Compared to previous generations, the concentration time of snowflakes is impaired due to the visual and sound demands of this century. Televisions, smartphones, smartwatches or street signs hijack their attention. This is the generation of the "notifyees". Their brains are constantly waiting for the next notification. Even during a conversation between two people who are physically close, one of them may have to take their smartphone to check if there is a notification. For the first time in the history of the human brain, what happens far away is more important than what happens in front of you. A young person today is able to interrupt a conversation with those around him to say "there was an earthquake in Indonesia, did you see it?

This lack of focus requires a review of the entire company's codes. The world must be adapted to these people whose attention must be constantly recaptured. For example, we must no longer make "slide shows" but "keynotes": these are speeches that are intended to keep the audience awake. We must no longer make "speeches" but "storytelling", i.e., wrapping the information we want to convey in a fascinating fictional story. Storytelling consists of trying to create one or more stories with strong seductive and convincing power within organizations or the public. These stories, which can be simple anecdotes or entire speeches, are used to convey complex messages more effectively, based on the principle that "emotion makes you more receptive".

In this ultra-connected world, there are attention thieves. It's the little useless notifications of everyday life like Facebook telling you "one of your friends is going to attend an event near you", LinkedIn asking you "have you thought about updating your profile this year?" or an online press application that tells you that "Neymar is going to change soccer clubs".

These brain time thieves should be eradicated. Although these applications are useful, it is important to enter the settings page of your phone to disable most of these notifications. Few notifications are important. Receiving a notification to learn that there is a failure on a RER line that you never take is totally stupid.

Resilience

In psychology, resilience is the phenomenon of being able to return from a state of post-traumatic stress. But without even going as far as the notion of stress or trauma, we can speak of resilience to qualify the ability to recover from an offence.

There are two ways of looking at it: either snowflakes have a longer list of topics that may offend them, or their ability to recover is weaker. It's probably even the sum of the two problems.

This generation, which is offended, irritated, sad or offended at the slightest event that does not go in their direction, is particularly made up of young people born after 1990, the "Millennials". A sub-group of snowflakes, the Millennials are the people who are defined as young enough to have always lived in the post-9/11 world. They have also always had a computer at home and don't remember life without the internet.

Not only do they hate to be offended, but they would like the world around them to take care of them! They can be caricatured as young people made of sugar, surrounded by bubble wrap, with tears in their eyes at all times.

It's because, having overprotected them, their parents forgot to prepare them for the constraints and the outside world. Their childhood is not a training session for adult life. On the contrary, their childhood is carefully crafted to surround them with a cocoon. When this cocoon breaks, usually in their mid-twenties, the shock is severe. They find themselves confronted with the character of others, the social backgrounds of others, the world of work, the business world in general, taxes, etc...

Journalist and writer Claire Fox says that the younger generation does not pretend to be fragile and shocked by everything. They really are because their parents and schools have removed all forms of risk and danger in their childhood. In France, for example, it is forbidden to bring a cake to classmates in kindergarten or elementary school if it is "home-made" because the preparation method and ingredients are unknown. In Scotland, a school wanted to change the color of its uniform, red, because it is suspected that the color red would make them hyperactive!

Unprepared for real life, snowflakes find themselves in great difficulty at work. They are asked to prove themselves while in childhood they were constantly praised by their parents. They are given a salary that afflicts them while their parents used to give them pocket money. They are asked to pay taxes when their parents never asked them to sweep a broom.

This generation does not like to be "criticized" or questioned. You might as well say that managers don't know where they stand. As this generation has started to take its place within companies, management codes are being shaken up little by little. Indeed, it is clearly not possible to "manage" them in the same way as the older generation! Whereas people who went to work in the 50/60s accepted their fate with philosophy by saying to themselves "I leave my life aside for 8 hours to earn my bread", the snowflake generation wants to come to the office with motivation and a big salary. Today's young adults don't put anything aside when they come to the office: they want to be treated with dignity, and to feel that they are truly producing something for the future of the world and the company as well as for their own future. We're not saying that's wrong, but it's new, anyway.

In order not to hurt their ego, managers must stop giving orders by subtly transforming them into advice. A current young person to whom they say "the work you gave me back is really lame! "comes home sobbing, pours his hatred for his boss on social networks, and then thinks about resigning. To avoid this, current managers (some of whom are already snowflakes) will opt instead for the phrase "It's really great what you've done but I'll show you what you can do to improve it by tomorrow".

The younger generations are also used to a regular form of reward. Video games, the school or parents are responsible for this permanent reward system. A child in the 90s never waits very long to be rewarded. When they arrive at the company, they expect the same treatment. When they are told "wait until next year for a raise," they are so upset that it feels like a year lasts a century.

Born largely after the telephone and shortly before the internet, snowflakes are very communicative. They can't stand the lack of response to an e-mail, which they consider a real affront. To avoid this, it is very important for companies to set up instant messaging and physical meetings.

The workplace should be a physical meeting place. Younger generations do not call it a "workplace" but see it as a "meeting place for colleagues". Companies have understood this and have therefore invented a new discipline: QWL. The "Quality of Life at Work" is the set of measures aimed at making the time spent in the workplace pleasant. Previous generations did not need it. Those born after 1990 demanded it: bright colors, good temperature in the offices, mineral water fountain, large windows, clean toilets, place to isolate oneself, rest room, table soccer, green plants, Wi-Fi, game console, cafeteria, free food are some of the wellness tricks that companies have put in place to attract and retain younger people. A function has even been created: happiness officer is the role of the person who implements these wellness features. In large companies, these people are led by a "Happiness Manager".

Work is the first place in their lives where their overprotective parents can no longer do anything for them. At school, they used to be able to get their parent to intervene against this institution. It is well known that since the 80s, parents have come to yell at (or hit) teachers when their child has a bad grade. Some children are even able to threaten a teacher with the phrase "I'm going to tell my parents", whereas in previous generations the threat was reversed: "If this continues, I'll tell your parents! The phrase "I'm going to tell my parents" shows a form of solidarity between adults. Once at work, the shock is severe and the parent can no longer do anything!

Outside of the professional context, the observation is the same. The snowflake wants to be stroked in the direction of the hair at all times. Instead of putting up with what society tells them, snowflake wants society to adapt to each individual to avoid hurting them. Stupid press articles with headlines like "I don't want kids, and I wish people would stop asking me for justifications" or "Our age makes you feel bad" are flourishing. These titles make me say "oh, poor cabbage living in a peaceful country, yes you there, in your couch with your iPhone in your hand, poor little cabbage".

In American universities, small groups of students claiming to be "vulnerable" claim that they might be "offended" by the comments made by a particular guest speaker, so that the speaker's intervention would be cancelled.

This generation raised far from wars, by parents who were themselves raised far from wars, literally whines for nothing, it must be admitted. Fortunately, one should not wish for the return of wars. But what happens to these people who spend their lives finding the world around them stressful, oppressive and aggressive?

These young people have goals. Life goals. Career goals. They find themselves frustrated by daily life. They say "I will have a yacht and no children". Others say, "When I'm thirty, I'll be married and have a big car. Or "I will be the director of a large company. But their parents forgot to remind them that it wasn't enough to want it to have it. Usually, the debacle occurs around age 30. From zero to 20, they were pampered. From 20 to 30, they had a hard time and found that "everyone was mean". At 30, they find themselves taking stock and saying "it didn't work out the way I wanted it to".

In a sense, it is the opposite of the thinking of the previous generation. They didn't believe in anything special and yet they did well in life. They built the world we live in today without having dreamed about it in advance, like Steve Jobs or Bill Gates. While the snowflake generation wants to become as rich as Bill Gates by working 35 hours per week and 200 days per year.

Tired of not doing exactly what they planned, snowflakes whine aloud but exult in their joy and replay or amplify their successes on social networks. They use their Instagram profile to showcase their restaurant meals or vacation trips. Their Facebook allow them to receive a shower of "Happy Birthday, baby!" Twitter allows them to assault others, while sitting comfortably in their bedroom. LinkedIn allows them to shine in front of the whole world by writing their resume. The "financial cashflow manager in a large multinational company" on LinkedIn is only just a cashier at McDonald's. The "blockchain and cryptocurrencies expert deputy" is a trainee and the "front-to-back equity derivatives portfolio management analyst" is a PHP developer.

In politics, snowflake is very involved. Rarely abstentionist, snowflake places deep hopes in the politician. The politician replaces the protective hand of parents. More than the previous generation, young people born after 1980 believe in the power of politicians to change their daily lives. He applies the complete opposite of JFK's famous phrase: "don't ask yourself what your country can do for you, but ask yourself what you can do for your country". Snowflake, for his country, he has absolutely nothing planned to do! It must be recognized that at the base of snowflake behavior there is something individualistic. Still nicknamed "generation I have the right", the snowflake generation tires society by its individualism which goes against the general interest. They proclaim the right "to have a smartphone in the classroom", the right to Wi-Fi, the right to write badly, the right to pay less, the right to claim their singularity.

In reality, after each election, the snowflake is unable to accept the defeat of its camp. After the election of Donald Trump or after the victory of Yes to Brexit, young Americans or British did what they know how to do best: whine and protest. Without any respect for electoral rules, they took to the streets to contest the result of the election or referendum. The Americans, in particular, used the slogan "Donald Trump is not my President". So, they believe they have the rules of the game.

On societal and animal issues, the snowflake generation tends to bury its head in the sand. Faced with disturbing information, they prefer to cover their ears and will even hold a grudge against the person providing the information. This posture reinforces good thinking. This generation is too young to develop a critical mind, so they opt, without thinking, for the most pleasant thoughts, whether true or false:

- Immigration is good,
- You have to be a vegetarian,
- All religions are pacifist,
- There are no difficult neighborhoods,
- Politicians are honest,
- Multiculturalism is great,
- Etc...

For illustration, I will take the example of chicken farms where small male chicks are crushed as soon as they are born because they are useless: their meat is not sought after and they do not lay eggs. This information may be painful to hear, but it is still true. It is precisely by knowing this that we can act or legislate. Not by hiding your eyes.

Resilience also lies in patience. Sometimes an embarrassing, exhausting or stressful situation is only temporary. To overcome them, there is sometimes nothing to do but wait. One hour. One day. One month. One year. But the brains of the younger generation go very fast and are not used to patience. Millennials live in instantaneity. They are born after the remote control, after the microwave oven, after the sign that indicates the waiting time for the subway or bus. They don't want to wait at all! Things that required effort in the past are accessible at the tip of the finger now, thanks to applications. You don't wait for a film to be shown on a specific date, you watch it on Netflix. You don't wait for a means of transportation; you order it on Uber. You don't look for a restaurant, you order on Deliveroo.

These applications and technologies are admirable, but again, we have to take a look at the big picture. We are not always consumers. Sometimes we have to be the opposite: creators. And a creator has to be patient. The snowflake generation should be reminded to be patient when there are no other choices. There are no applications to speed up pregnancy (or to get pregnant). There are no applications to heal faster from an illness. So, you have to learn to recognize what depends on technology and what does not.

Cultural appropriation

One of the battle horses of snowflakes is the fight against cultural appropriation. This term acquires a negative connotation, popular in the American cultural landscape, and tends to be imported in French-speaking countries. Cultural appropriation thus sometimes today refers to the idea that the use of elements of a culture by members of a "dominant" culture would be intrinsically disrespectful and would constitute a form of oppression and spoliation. This concept is in direct conflict with the propensity of cultures to feed off one another, making cultures moving and malleable over time. We then speak of interculturality. As an example, the American saga Star Wars was inspired by elements of Akira Kurosawa's The Hidden Fortress, itself inspired by elements of Shakespeare's work.

Since the 2010's, it would seem that it is forbidden for a person of culture A to benefit from the customs of a person of culture B. This is a form of identity hypersensitivity never seen in human history.

The phrase used by snowflakes to illustrate their fight against cultural appropriation is "My culture is not your prom dress" which translates into French as "Ma culture ne doit pas être ta robe de bal".

This sentence was born in the land of snowflakes, the United States, a country that has a hard time living in harmony with its cultures and ethnic groups (races, they say over there). At the end of each school year, Americans are used to participate in a prom, which is a general evening for all high school students. On this occasion, the girls wear, sometimes for the first time in their lives, a beautiful dress (the prom dress). This is where the trouble starts: each girl must be extremely careful to wear a dress that is "in tune" with her own culture, at the risk of being immediately labeled racist or "cultural appropriation". This is what happened, on April 23, 2018, to a young white American girl who did not feel the flood of insults she would get from wearing a pretty red silk dress. You know, this is the "qipao" also called the "cheongsam", a very beautiful traditional Chinese silk dress. Made in one piece, it is usually quite tight and slit on the sides. Keziah, 18 years old, is radiant for this evening, next to her boyfriend. She posts the object of her pride, a picture of her wearing the said dress, on Twitter. A few minutes later, a first remark falls on her: "My culture does NOT have to be your fucking prom dress! "tells her what appears to be a Chinese-American. Surprised, the girl replies, "I answer those who provoke too much negativity: I have no contempt for Chinese culture. I just wanted to show my admiration for this culture. I refuse to delete this photo because I have done nothing wrong. It's just a dress.... And it is beautiful."

On September 4, 2018, it starts again. The young Megan Barton Hanson is shown in photo on Instagram, her hair braided. Apparently, the fact that she is white is a problem. A verbal battle rages over her post: some insult her, others accuse her of showing a deep contempt for black women. Luckily, some users keep a cool head and take her side.

Famous women do not escape the phenomenon: Katy Perry disguised as a geisha, Kylie Jenner in braids, Karlie Kloss wearing an American Indian headdress, Selena Gomez with a tilak (small red dot on the forehead of Indian women), Beyoncé disguised as an Indian, etc...

In the United States, during the year 2016, mothers are worried about the violence that their daughters might suffer if they were to dress them up as little Moana (a Polynesian character).

The costume stores, don't know how to react anymore! Dressing up in a traditional costume from another country is their business.

This concept of the crime of cultural appropriation is a new foolishness on the part of young Americans, but one that will gradually spread to France. There will be no escaping it.

The ethnic groups most likely to be affected are Blacks, Asians and Polynesians. The first do not support any more that white women want to wear braids. The second consider that they have the monopoly of the silk clothing and the third are irritated by the fashion of the Polynesian tattoos worn by the whites.

These outraged reactions from snowflakes show how terrible racists they can become. A form of soft totalitarianism takes hold of them: the snowflake, by its outraged look, becomes itself an aggressor, especially on social networks.

It would be interesting to return the concept of cultural appropriation to its own detractors by asking them to remove from their daily lives everything that is not native to their culture. By this I mean suppressing their morning espresso, their lunch hamburger, their Chanel bag, their croissants. But also banning people from eating sushi, banning hair straightening, banning tartan patterns outside of Scotland, banning breast surgery, etc... If we don't pay attention to this stupid phenomenon, tanning will be forbidden to whites and curling iron will be forbidden to Asians. For St. Patrick's Day, there will be only Irish in the street.

The situation could become much more ridiculous in the coming years. There is even a risk of a kind of identity backlash that will hurt everyone. If white people one day start reminding the world of all that European cultures have brought to humanity (sometimes forcibly, sometimes not), we will have a very bad time.

This movement of cultural anti-appropriation must be stopped as a matter of urgency, and even the mixing of the world's different cultures must be accelerated and celebrated.

Their children

It's clear that snowflakes are children who are ill-prepared for adult life. But when they themselves become parents, what will they do?

First of all, on humor, in my opinion, it is likely that the line of self-censorship will continue. It is hard to imagine that Western society will turn back the clock. Humor is losing ground day after day, sacrificed on the altar of good sense. This movement seems irreversible to me. Humorists have to walk on eggshells to do their job. They already have to avoid talking about skin color, religion, corpulence, handicaps, nationalities, homosexuality, the poor, women, male-female relations. In the future, their ground will be even more mined. In 2018, the public debate is beginning to become more tense on subjects that would have been unimaginable just a few years ago:

- Vegetarianism,
- The origin of first names,
- Kissing a woman on the cheeks when you meet her for the first time,
- Spanking for children,
- Separation of men's and women's toilets,
- Regional accents,
- Satirical news sites,
- Learning Arabic at school,
- Gender theory,
- The concept of cultural appropriation,

- Animal acts in circuses.

It is likely that society is becoming more and more tense about everything and nothing. By emptying all humor and public debate of its substance, only the idiots will be left in the face of good sense. The others will turn to paid outlets. Free or overly open media such as television, websites, subway ads or big Parisian shows will be devoid of depth.

The uncensored debate will be hidden behind private and/or paid platforms such as Netflix or HBO. Already nowadays, to laugh at a sketch of Les Inconnus or Coluche, one has to turn to YouTube because television no longer wants to hear about these "racists".

On the other hand, due to their lack of resilience, snowflakes are likely to give their children a totally different education than the one they received. Shameful to have been so lacking in courage as adults, today's snowflakes will not repeat the same mistakes with their children. They will prepare them much better for life. They will raise them "the hard way" by telling them "you know me, I suffered too much when I was a young adult so I have to educate you severely". It will come full circle.

The snowflake generation can also be seen positively. Because of its fragility, this generation has more chances to succeed in reducing discrimination, violence and pollution than its predecessors. We can hope, thanks to them, for a less brutal world. We can hope for a decrease in acts of violence such as, for example, school harassment. As a result, we can imagine a decrease in mental problems related to post-traumatic stress.

Anti-snowflakes

The snowflake generation cannot be generalized to all people born after 1980. Among them, many are beginning to be annoyed by the fragility of their fellow snowflake riders.

On the Web, the wave of indignation of snowflakes is parodied and mocked by people of the same age.

For a yes or no, snowflakes say they are "shocked", "offended", "hurt" or "outraged". To that, others respond with a squeaky sense of humor: "I'm offended that you are offended".

Others remain incredulous and write "And one day, without knowing why, we became shocked by everything and anything".

The snowflake has even become a Halloween disguise: it consists of a transparent bubble wrap t-shirt with "Fragile" and "Handle with Care" labels stuck on it. You have to add a "I'm offended" cap and walk softly with a sulky pout.

This counterculture, more cynical, less fragile, exists within the Y and Z generations themselves. It finds its rallying point on social networks or on the sarcastic humorous site 9gag.com.

On some anti-snowflakes memes, you can see a young man going to see a psychologist because his teacher or employer said something to him that upset him. The therapist says, "Okay, I'm going to prescribe a pair of testicles for you.

Others lament: "We live in a generation of emotionally weak people. Everything has to be sanitized because it's offensive, even the truth."

In literature, the author Trey Willis has released in 2014, the book "The Snowflake Effect - How the self-esteem movement ruined a generation".

Journalist Claire Fox wrote the book 'I Find That Offensive! (I Find That Offensive!) to criticize the drifting of snowflakes.

Sources

Article "The snowflake generation: so difficult to manage?"
https://www.myrhline.com/actualite-rh/la-generation-snowflake-egalement-difficile-a-manager.html

Wikipedia page of "Generation (sociology)".
https://fr.wikipedia.org/wiki/G%C3%A9n%C3%A9r ation_(sociology)

Wikipedia page of "Wilhelm Dilthey".
https://fr.wikipedia.org/wiki/Wilhelm_Dilthey

Fight Club" Wikipedia page
https://fr.wikipedia.org/wiki/Fight_Club_(movie)

Fight Club" movie
https://www.amazon.fr/Fight-club-Brad-Pitt/dp/B00005AV4N/ref=sr_1_2?s=dvd&ie=UTF8&qid=1543080922&sr=1-2&keywords=fight+club

Wikipedia page of "Victorian morality".
https://en.wikipedia.org/wiki/Victorian_morality

Wikipedia page of "Helicopter Parent".
https://fr.wikipedia.org/wiki/Parent_h%C3%A9licopt%C3%A8re

Article ""EVEN THE BLACK WORD BECOMES TABOO, IT'S PURE FOLIE"""

https://next.liberation.fr/vous/2007/12/10/meme-
le-mot-noir-devient-tabou-c-est-de-la-pure-
folie_108193

Sketch of strangers "The hospital
https://www.youtube.com/watch?v=RFLxu5_m3r8

Wikipedia page of "Generation Snowflake".
https://en.wikipedia.org/wiki/Generation_Snowflak
e

Blackface" Wikipedia page
https://fr.wikipedia.org/wiki/Blackface

Wikipedia page of "Vaiana, the Legend of the End of
the World
https://fr.wikipedia.org/wiki/Vaiana,_la_L%C3%A9
gende_du_bout_du_monde#R%C3%A9actions_sur_la
_repr%C3%A9sentation_des_cultures_polyn%C3%A9
siennes

Homosexuality" Wikipedia page
https://fr.wikipedia.org/wiki/Homosexualit%C3%A
9

Grossophobia" Wikipedia page
https://fr.wikipedia.org/wiki/Grossophobie

Article "Individualism, rejection of authority... Survey
on the "I have the right" generation"
http://www.leparisien.fr/fait-du-
jour/individualisme-rejet-de-l-autorite-enquete-sur-
la-generation-j-ai-le-droit-16-01-2018-7502937.php

Wikipedia page of "List of French Ministers of
Ecology".

https://fr.wikipedia.org/wiki/Liste_des_ministres_fr
an%C3%A7ais_de_l%27%C3%89cologie

Wikipedia page of "Society for the Protection of
Animals
https://fr.wikipedia.org/wiki/Soci%C3%A9t%C3%A
9_protectrice_des_animaux

Band Aid" Wikipedia page
https://fr.wikipedia.org/wiki/Band_Aid

We Are the World" Wikipedia page
https://fr.wikipedia.org/wiki/We_Are_the_World

Wikipedia page of "Don't Touch My Buddy
https://fr.wikipedia.org/wiki/Touche_pas_%C3%A0
_mon_pote

Wikipedia page of "Les Restos du cœur" (The Rest of
the Heart)
https://fr.wikipedia.org/wiki/Les_Restos_du_c%C5
%93ur

Wikipedia page of "Children's Rights".
https://fr.wikipedia.org/wiki/Droits_de_l%27enfant

Public Life Site
http://www.vie-publique.fr/politiques-
publiques/politique-handicap/chronologie/

Article ""Coolest monkey in the jungle": H&M
apologizes for controversial photo".
https://www.rtbf.be/info/societe/detail_coolest-
monkey-in-the-jungle-h-m-presente-ses-excuses-
pour-une-photo-polemique?id=9805553

Article ""Every year, nearly 50 million chicks are
culled"".
https://www.lemonde.fr/planete/article/2015/08/1
0/des-parlementaires-se-mobilisent-contre-le-
broyage-de-poussins-vivants_4719250_3244.html

Article "Is our generation "maladjusted" to the world
of work? The brilliant analysis of Simon Sinek"
http://www.madmoizelle.com/millenials-monde-
travail-simon-sinek-698609

Youtube video "The racist advertising of the Chinese
laundry Qiaobi (May 2016)".
https://www.youtube.com/watch?v=lT6AZX55ZGE

Wikipedia page of "Silent Generation".
https://fr.wikipedia.org/wiki/G%C3%A9n%C3%A9r
ation_silencieuse

Wikipedia page of "Baby Boomers
https://en.wikipedia.org/wiki/Baby_boomers

Generation X" Wikipedia page
https://fr.wikipedia.org/wiki/G%C3%A9n%C3%A9r
ation_X

Lost Generation" Wikipedia page
https://fr.wikipedia.org/wiki/G%C3%A9n%C3%A9r
ation_perdue

Wikipedia page of "Generation Y".
https://fr.wikipedia.org/wiki/G%C3%A9n%C3%A9r
ation_Y

Generation Z" Wikipedia page
https://en.wikipedia.org/wiki/Generation_Z

Wikipedia page of "Storytelling (technique)".
https://fr.wikipedia.org/wiki/Storytelling_(technical)

Offended Millennial Costume
https://me.me/i/im-offended-ragi-millennial-fragile-fwd-my-halloween-costume-was-3726178

Wikipedia page of "Cultural Appropriation".
https://fr.wikipedia.org/wiki/Appropriation_culturelle

Article "My culture is not your prom dress: US teen's qipao sparks 'cultural appropriation' row on Twitter"
https://www.thestar.com.my/news/world/2018/05/02/my-culture-is-not-your-prom-dress-us-teens-qipao-sparks-cultural-appropriation-row-on-twitter/#yUA03mutP3i1zyVw.99"

Article "Katy Perry's kiss to 19-year-old American Idol candidate causes controversy".
https://www.20minutes.fr/television/2238031-20180315-video-bisou-katy-perry-candidat-american-idol-19-ans-fait-polemique

Article "Generation Snowflake: how we train our kids to be censorious cry-babies"
https://www.spectator.co.uk/2016/06/generation-snowflake-how-we-train-our-kids-to-be-censorious-cry-babies/

Article "Eastern Primary red uniform kept despite claims it made kids hyper"
https://www.eveningtelegraph.co.uk/fp/eastern-primary-red-uniform-kept-despite-claims-made-kids-hyper/

The Author

Lionel Bolnet is a French computer engineer and writer, born July 14, 1984. He is also the author of:

- The Maldives,
- Las Vegas: History and Architecture,
- Understanding Sybase ASE 15.7,
- Backup your files.

Due to his personal experience and age, he can be considered the snowflake he knows best.